First

Course

in

Turbulence

PITT POETRY SERIES

Ed Ochester, Editor

First
Course
in
Turbulence

DEAN YOUNG

University of Pittsburgh Press

Published by the University of Pittsburgh Press, Pittsburgh, Pa. 15261
Copyright © 1999, Dean Young

Manufactured in the United States of America
Printed on acid-free paper
10 9 8 7 6 5 4 3 2

Acknowledgments are located at the end of this book.

The publication of this book is supported by a grant from the Pennsylvania Council on the Arts.

for Kevin Stein,
Mary Ruefle,
Cornelia Nixon

Big Subject. *Big Shadow.*

—ROBERT HASS

Contents

three

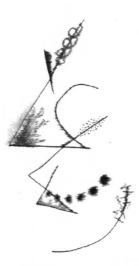

one

If Thou Dislik'st What Thou First Light'st On

I had come to the house, in a cave of trees,
I had dreamed of the perfect gray pants,
I have a life that did not become,
a young sister made of glass.
I have done it again.
I like a church, I like a cowl,
I like the look of agony.
I love the old melodious lays,
I love it when they demonstrate the oxygen masks,
never messing up their hair.
I met the Bishop on the road,
In a coign of the cliff between high and low,
In a dark time,
Among wolves and periwinkles,
In a station of the metro,
In Breughel's great painting, *The Kermess.*
Indeed I must confess,
Indigo, magenta, color of ghee,
what the hell is the color of ghee?
In June amid the golden fields,
In some unused lagoon, some nameless bay,
In spite of all the learned say,
In the depths of the Greyhound station,
In this world, this isle of dreams,
Intimations of mortality,
In unexpected infancy,
In vain, in vain—the all composing hours.
Yadda yadda yadda.
I saw the best minds of my generation et cetera,
I saw spiders marching through the air
but let's skip this part, okay?

The usual taste of liquor never brewed,
the usual It is June, it is June,
it is ten years since we rowed,
it is 12:20 in New York a Friday
but seems it out of battle I escaped
and now I wander lonely as a cloud.
I was angry with a friend,
I went into the public 'ouse for a pint o' beer,
I went to the Garden of Love
but I wonder, do you feel today as I do
caught in an index's apparatus of a thousand
versions of myself but not sure I even exist?
Dawns and hangovers and phone calls,
nothing but silence on the other end.
All this fog, a jar in Tennessee, torches
going out. Go down any road far enough
and you'll come to a slaughterhouse,
but keep going and you'll reach the sea.

The Infirmament

An end is always punishment for a beginning.
If you're Catholic, sadness is punishment
for happiness, you become the bug you squash
if you're Hindu, a flinty space opens
in your head after a long night of laughter
and wine. For waking there are dreams,
from French poetry, English poetry,
for light fire although sometimes
fire must be punished by light
which is why psychotherapy had to be invented.
A father may say nothing to a son for years.
A wife may keep something small folded deep
in her underwear drawer. Clouds come in
resembling the terrible things we believe
about ourselves, a rock comes loose
from a ledge, the baby just cries
and cries. Doll in a chair,
windshield wipers, staring off
into the city lights. For years
you may be unable to hear the word *monkey*
without a stab in the heart because
she called you that the summer she thought
she loved you and you thought you loved
someone else and everyone loved
your salad dressing. And the daffodils
come up in the spring and the snow covers
the road in winter and the water covers
the deep trenches in the sea where all the time
the inner stuff of this earth surges up
which is how the continents are made
and broken.

The Unattainable

Often, those first years of divorce,
his car windows are smashed. Often
in this case is thrice but I
can imagine often being once. Mouse
in a trap. Fire sky. Heard shot. He
lives in a minor key of fear but
also a lot in bed with a new woman
met one yellow day on the labyrinthine
passageways where only the cyclists
seem to know where they're going,
endangering those who don't. Safety
catch, melted crayon, broken string.
When she steps from the pool of her
uniform, her breasts . . . well, who
wouldn't sense the quick exhaustion
of descriptive language seeing those breasts,
say Parthenon? say comet? say lion running?
but luckily along comes Breton with
"handkerchiefs drying on a rosebush"
which is truer to the spirit than
any actual appearance. Bones of a canary.
Destiny. Often beauty is disguised
by appearance just as music can be
by sound, the dreaming wish by the waking
wish until there's this terrible stress
because a thing must finally reveal itself,
break itself. Leaning shadow, cinder
heart, shouts. In Gorky's *The Unattainable,*
the line begins to free itself from any
utility of contour and becomes a trajectory.
One day, Gorky hung himself from a beam

but left us in charge of these ravishments.
Hello, interior of the sun. Usually alone
on Sundays, she won't get off until late,
the man steams rice because it's cheap
and easy and feels in its austerity poetic
like candles during a power outage
or trying on overcoats all afternoon,
buying none. Chosen feather, smoke smudge,
red parabola within flesh.

Acceptance Speech

This time I'm not going to say a thing
about deity. It's not the blizzard,
it's three days after. Trinkle from thawing
roofs, ruined crocus pronging through.
Ruin, I promise, won't be mentioned again.
Trees, sure, still begging in the road, split
to the bole but this isn't about the chainsaw.
A pruning saw will have to do. The puppets
aren't hanging themselves in each other's
strings. Everyone's easily identifiable
beneath the funny mask. Somewhere in Oregon,
Mary has another month to go, she's comfortable
in any position for thirty-five seconds. Lulu,
we know you're in there but no one's
blaming you for reluctance to come out.
Poetry is the grinding of a multiplicity
throwing off sparks, wrote Artaud
and look what that got him: toothlessness
and shock therapy. Your dad, who has the worst
teeth of anyone I know, once ordered eggplant
in a steakhouse. Do not order eggplant
in a steakhouse turned out to be more
than aphoristicly true. Do not spend a lot
of time in an asylum writing cruel poems
if you can help it, one Artaud is enough.
In Kandinsky's *Blue 2*, there's a shape
in two rows of shapes that seems okay
although to the right's a capsized canoe
full of mathematicians, to the left a bow
about to launch the killer astrolabe.
By what manner is the soul joined to

the body? How about climbing a ladder
of fire? No thanks. On TV, a rhino's
lying in some red dust, munching a thorn.
You wouldn't think he could ejaculate
for half an hour straight, but you'd be wrong.
See that cloud, it might weigh 10,000 pounds
which is about average for a cloud.
Happy birthday, happy birthday to you.
Tony says Mary is always writing about the sacred.
Talcum powder, binoculars, this decimated
planet. I know, a promise has been made
but Tony's been sick for years and no one
knows with what. Flax oil, bark tinctures,
corticosteroids. He's not exactly someone
you'd trust to drive your car, but still.
Something awful's coming, isn't it?
Would it help if I said Amen?

Tiger

Look of a wren, not dead yet,
I pick up to save from the cats,
look I recognize as my Dad's after
they've taken his glasses and teeth,
what world was he leaving me unbequeathed,
look of a thing unresigned, about to be eaten,
what question am I still too late asking?

And because I know no one will be consoled
or absolved or cured, blossoms
fall upon me from drenched trees
in recompense. Aqueous nimbus
blazing the street, azure uncouplings of clouds
and whatever survives thinks it's flower forever,
flame forever jackknifing through
the dispersed ions of William Blake.

Today, there are tigers everywhere, even
the waitress who brings the large juice
carries a punctured heart, even the carpet
is a tongue. Apparently none of us
are maimed enough, one body a permanent
kneel, another a boat, red leak in its chest,

one this wrecked lacewing, eyes flecked
from some pulverized jewel, antenna so long,
so attenuated, what vibration, what pheromone
won't drive each crazy with the need to be loved,
to be eaten? At what point did I leave

those crowded rooms, what am I hunting for?

One door won't open, one opens on more
doors, one upon fire gushing a plasmic
light as if from some sliced-open orange
because only so much can be absorbed,
converted into sugars. Mist staggers over
the grass like the spirit over the whole

corporeal mess those first hesitant seconds
after death, jamming the radio signals,
hey-na, sha-la while the orderlies lean
on their brooms. If the knife is in you,
it may be best not to pull it out. Perhaps

if I just carried you into the sea.
I know someone could make a great weapon of me
if only I was thrown hard enough.

Warbler

My novelist is suffering from an unknown.
She sits at her desk weeping
and her tears are as rain upon my elephant skull.
After eroticism, suffering is my favorite subject.
What is her skin made of?
A lot of water doesn't come close to explaining it.
The writing is on the wrong side of the wall.
Sometimes I go in there with a dust rag
and there's a warbler outside her window.
Maybe yellow rumped. Maybe titular.
Fucking bird, trying to ruin it for everyone.
It sings: hapless gyroscope, hunka
burning, I melt the snow.
How should I know?
We must all disappear somewhere.
First you will be sitting at your desk
then you will be standing beside yourself
and it will no longer be as if you are trying
to open a door and unable,
trying to speak and unable,
not knowing the trees that have always roamed there,
not knowing the rain that has always fallen
and the conditional will no longer masquerade
as certainty and your childhood pleading
will not return.
The problem isn't that you will become dust
but that you ever thought you aren't already.
I believe she will be able to use all this
all this she
at some point she may be able to use all this
maybe half of this as material.

In this day and age, there can be no composition
without decomposition. Sometimes I wish
I had the strength to drink a cup of coffee.
It is not night, it's just dark.
Sometimes I wish I had the strength
to really clean this place. Vacuum inside
the elephant skull, move all the furniture,
even her tympanic desk which was made
by her grandfather from the breastbones
of broken boats. Not a single nail.
Once he rode a horse through his own kitchen.
Later he was surrounded by a beautiful sphere of light.

He Said Turn Here

and then Tony showed us the lake
where he had thrown some of his sadness last summer
and it had dissolved like powder
so he thought maybe the lake could take
some of the radiant, aluminum kind
he had been making lately.
And it did.
It was a perfect lake,
none of the paint had chipped off,
no bolts showing, the arms that Dante
and Virgil would have to hack through
not even breaking the surface.
Mumbling Italian to itself,
it had climbed down two wooden stairs
back to the beach now that the rains were done.
How strange to be water so close to the ocean
yet the only other water you get to talk to
comes from the sky. Maybe this is why
it seems so willing to take on
Tony's sadness which sometimes corrodes
his friends, which is really
many different sadnesses, smaller
and smaller, surrounded by more
and more space, each a world and
at its core an engine like a bee
inside a lily, like buzzing inside
the bee. It seems like nothing
could change its color although
we couldn't tell what color it was,
it kept changing. In the summer,
Tony says he comes down early each day

and there's no one around so the lake
barely says a thing when he dives in
and once when his kitchen was on fire in Maine
and he was asleep, the lake came and bit his hand,
trying to drag him to safety
and some nights in New Mexico,
he can hear it howling,
searching for him in the desert
so we're glad Tony has this lake
and we promise to come back in August
and swim with him across,
maybe even race.

Bird Sanctuary

For a while we didn't know what to call it
but we were all after it so we had to call it something.
Seen Vladimir? we started asking in metal shop.
Vladimir, we'd say, watching the first snow.
Was it longing for something in our childhood
or was it the sense of the world made new
and ready for our ruin? If you were Achilles,
it was either sulking in your tent or
struggling with a strange river.
Vladimir, it turns out, is entirely
in the mind. Well, maybe.
A guy I used to shoplift with
once made a model of the Eiffel Tower
out of sugar cubes but halfway through
he realized toothpicks
would have been a more expressive medium.
The Vladimir was gone but when he finished
and got his B+ anyway, we put it out
in the rain and the Vladimir returned
as it dissolved. *Wabi* some Japanese poet
called it, wondering why Americans paint
their barns when it takes years of exposure
to get them to look so full of *wabi*.
At first there was an actual Vladimir
on space station Mir watching ants trying
to behave in zero gravity but when
his nose clogged up, Igor replaced him.
Imagine sneezing inside a space helmet.
Theoretical scientists spend a lot of time
colliding things, trying to locate Vladimir
until half decide Vladimir doesn't exist

so there's a big feud about funding.
During the past, Vladimir was called
phlogiston and everyone and thing had it,
especially if you burst into silver flames.
Imagine being a tree made into a thousand
matchsticks. Once on a ferry going to Larkspur,
we stood in the spray watching fog paw through the city.
Even now, we love each other.

Sky Dive

In school it had been important to learn
the names of battleships, diseases, museums,
kings, the internal scheme of the squid
which is called taxonomy but outside, in the fields,
it seemed most important to know the names
of sex organs: vulva, Mount Olympus,
anadromous pod and that was called soccer practice.
Beside me in Earth Science sat Debbie
until she was killed by a Volkswagen
so the rest of the year I did the experiments
alone. Say crack my fingers backwards, she whispered
while I tried to organize plastic seashells.
The earth had folded into itself many times.
Ann, Jill, Brenda, Elizabeth. Kinesis,
the golgi apparatus, the ellipsis. Give up,
go to bed, dream. Then to wake up twenty years later
after a party knowing you behaved perfectly
shamefully, the brain is threatened sea life,
astronomers predict discs of dust hold clues
to the birth of the universe and then to make tea
and telephone apologies. What was her name,
the one by the door? Expostulations of orange juice.
Purple clouds. Twice I jumped from an airplane
to forget a beautiful woman who was sleeping
with some guy instead of me who made guitars
from scratch. Handprints on an aquarium,
tissue paper. Irregular envelopes. To begin,
each player selected a game piece. She was
beautiful and drunk but not as drunk
as her dress which kept hailing cabs
even at the party. Beneath the clothing

is the skin and beneath the skin, viscera, bones
but beneath that there is just the skin
of the other side so clearly something
is unaccounted for. Green river,
lobelia, lightbulb shaped like a flame,
a chair shaped like a shoe. The last time
I landed, I forgot all I learned
throwing myself from a practice flight of stairs.
It drove me crazy, the way she smiled
at strangers and I could never be
a stranger. A thousand feet above the earth,
hanging from a handkerchief.

Familiar Territory

In the place I'm renting
the landlady must have thought the mess
hung on the wall was art but it's not nearly
messy enough, the suffering keeps leaking through,

the tragic human essence. One thing
we must eradicate, wrote Picabia,
is the expression of human essence
but just look at his distraught machinery,

gears ripping out their hair, pulleys
that can't even get out of bed,
brave little soldiers in a wrong war.
So what *is* the proper field procedure here?

To gently apply the forceps to the thoracic bulge
or just rip the sucker out by the wings?
Should A stay with B even though B
can't help what she feels for C

and why won't C answer his phone?
Sometimes you're the prince hearing of the king's demise,
sometimes the friend who must be hung as example
but who hasn't looted at least one church,

yanked the chalice through a beloved's ribs?
See this glove of thorns? Try it on.
See this ladder, it's made of ice.
So part of A says, Let's kill ourselves

but it's the same part that wants to eat a swan.
So part of me says, Let's go into town
and try on all manner of black velvet thing
but that's a line stolen from Mary's poem

which I love but don't understand.
I can't help myself from loving what I can't
stanza break
understand. Whatever you ask for, you're given

stanza break
something else. Instead of raspberry sherbet,
here's a mouthful of blood. Instead of a trip
to Italy, here's a statue of Shiva

but who isn't momentarily calmed by
the ornamental quality of all those weapons
in all those arms as if our ruin
was just interior decor:

all these heads sprouting from one head,
the corsage bursting from the chest,
grass growing from the father's mouth,
our mothers no longer recognizing us.

Petals in a river, ruby dropped in flames.
If you love me, now'd be a good time to say.
On the avenue, one sign vows,
I can write your name on a grain of rice.

The Invention of Heaven

The mind becomes a field of snow
but then the snow melts and dandelions
blink on and you can walk through them,
your trousers plastered with dew.
They're all waiting for you but first
here's a booth where you can win

a peacock feather for bursting a balloon,
a man in huge stripes shouting about
a boy who is half swan, the biggest
pig in the world. Then you will pass
tractors pulling other tractors,
trees snagged with bright wrappers

and then you will come to a river
and then you will wash your face.

Tribe

The first people came out of the lake
and their god was the raven. Craving
over the mitochondrial plain. The second people
came out of the volcano and their god,
the shark, ate the raven so the first people
turned orange and died. Song gone, dance
done. No one is sure where the third people
came from but they didn't last long.
Somehow they learned to turn themselves
into toads to frighten their enemies
but the toads couldn't pronounce the spells
to turn themselves back into people
and to this day you can still hear them trying.
This is where Wagner got his ideas.
Then the shark god gave birth to the coyote
and the whistling ant who mated with a cloud
and gave birth to the hawk and they all
battled and intermarried so the second people
invented the drum as a way of participating.
It was the drumming that brought forth
the fourth people who thought it was important
to always be elsewhere, searching for
some purple root, some flashy feather
for the hat's brim so most of them

were squashed by trucks when they wandered
onto the interstate at night. By then
the second people were pretty sick of
each other and they dreamed of mating
with fish, with lightning in puzzling
contortions, woke up, and to their credit,

wrote everything down. Then they would gather
in their condominiums, sharing descriptions
and disagreeing about the use of color and
whether a shovel could symbolize fear of intimacy.
But then it rained and the earth was covered
with water which was bad but not as bad
as when it gets covered with fire which
everyone knows is going to happen next.
Everywhere you look was once a sea and
in the sea grew gigantic serpents and
in their bellies precious stones and
inside the stones the eggs of another people
and inside these people, well, you get the idea.
Nothing is ever finished and nothing ever
perishes completely, there is always some
residue. Sometimes, in the dust, a cape clasp.
Sometimes, a rat. Everywhere are carved trees,
buried nameplates, initialed cliffs but

the earth, like a fox in a trap, is never done
gnawing itself just as the gods are never done
bickering and swallowing each other, jealous
of our beauty and ability to die.
No claim lasts.
Flags flapping in breeze become breeze.
Eyesight turns into starlight.
And this is how you've come to be
struggling with cellophane, smashing
the ham sandwich within. Human, sometimes
a stone washes up covered with clues. Sometimes
a tree gets knocked over by wind and inside is a flint
but how can you know what to ask or answer
when you don't even know who you are.

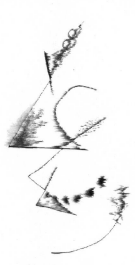

two

Only One of My Deaths

Because it seems the only way to save the roses
is to pluck the Japanese beetles out of
their convoluted paradise
and kill them, I think for a moment,
instead of crushing them in the driveway,
of impaling them on the thorns.
Perhaps they'd prefer that.

And Because Her Face

And because her face has finally flown
from the faces of strangers and I no longer
sleep in the room with her dresses,
the puppets and desiccated rose,
perhaps now her accusations are done,
that I forget her so now I can forget her,
betray her each time I don't find her lips
inside a peach after one bite, by running
on the ridge as if in celebration, shoulder
to shoulder with hawks, men radioing
their model planes in and out of the fog
as if anything could be given then taken back
from opacity, as if its absorptions could be
toyed with because the heart is a fearless
seething, throwing itself at the rocks
as if each wave had this grand idea
none had ever had about throwing itself
against some rocks, it seems nearly comic,
seems it could never stop and all that we love
we heave from ourselves and all that we love
is restored only transformed, broken like
a Roman statue where the head of the last
emperor, that madman, is removed, head
of the next, that madman, affixed, you can
barely make out a choker of cracks, slight
shift in stone's hue at the neck, our handiwork
has become so adroit and because I'm looking
at a cloud and not seeing a fist, her face
in flames, not seeing for once a chariot
and I've had something to eat, some carrots
and cheese, I thought I was through

with this part of my instruction, I thought
the head was done singing in the furnace and
I'd be able to sit in the dark again, at least
long enough for a movie, something with a starlet
clothed only in rain, some exploding planes
and when I came out it would be cooler,
smell of hay, cicadas splitting their bodies
with larger bodies, the beggars for an hour fed,
silent, nearly drunk enough, nearly satisfied
that all they've raved about has come to pass.

Colophon

More than the beetles turned russet,
sunset, dragging their shield, more than
the crickets who think it's evening all afternoon,
it's the bees I love this time of year.

Sated, maybe drunk, who've lapped at the hips
of too many flowers for one summer but
still must go on hunting, one secret
closing, another ensuing, picking

lock after lock, rapping the glass,
getting stuck in a puddle of dish soap,
almost winter, almost dark, reading far past
the last paragraph into the back blank page,

acknowledgments, and history of type.
I think when my head finally cracks
out will come one of those ravening scouts
autumnal with hunger beyond any sipping,

swallowing, beyond the hive's teeming
factory's needs. I think maybe then,
when I'm dying like a bug in a puddle
of dish soap, I'll be relieved,

my wings wet capes and not working,
antennae slicked back and not working,
eye that sees the ruby above going out,
eye that sees the ruby within getting brighter

as I drag myself to a tomato ripening
on the window sill, reddest, softest
island of my last planet, last aureola,
stinger waving and useless. I'll wait then,

while air from the north rushes gulf air,
a tree indicating wildly, each leaf woke
in orange outcry. It won't be suffering,
exactly. Rain coming, then gone, a chill

that means all my barbarous kind are alone
and perishing, our unrecognizable young
buried and waiting, bodies of fire becoming
bodies of air. I don't think there's any way

to prepare.

Maybe It Meant Something Else

(AFTER KENNETH KOCH)

when the little girl held forward her lamb
and called I love you. Maybe it meant
I love this lamb when she said I love you
to the man she'd never seen before
on the Greek island. She must have
learned the English during the war,
the resistance and counter-resistance.
Maybe someone with her mother. Maybe
it meant over here fleece you over there.
She seemed too young for it to mean poor us.
What spilled wine doesn't become only stain?
What kiss a winter, day a longing, ocean
a search, music a silence, music a scratch?
Where can I write your name? How can I
convince you I noticed and cared and loved you?
Atoms, all of it atoms becoming the atoms
of something else, an eyelash the leg
of a butterfly, a flake of skin
taken up into bark. Rocks,
an island almost entirely of rocks.
Cliffs with persuasive drops. Wine
that tastes like rope. Maybe she meant
only hello but part of him felt suddenly
grabbed from above as if by an old god
and that it'd be summer forever and
part of him felt his life just beginning
and that he'd died this way before,
weighed down with the memory of someone
long ago saying I love you
on a night he first realized

the sound of crickets was actually
many different sounds. It was all a gift,
he knew that even then, but
he thought you got to keep a gift,
thought that's what made them gifts
so when he shouted back, waving,
I love you too,
he wasn't exactly sure what it meant
so he needed to say it a hundred times more
which he did when he got back to his rooms
where his wife was bathing the baby
in a small, galvanized tub.

Lives of the Inventors

When Leonardo is 11 and still sober,
he brings home a dead wren to disconnect.
His parents hope he is a genius and not
just another morbid little boy dressed funny:
balloony pants, purple shoes, poofy hat.
They hope his brain isn't the Devil's
cricket. We shouldn't laugh. Back then
backwards handwriting was a scary thing.
People died from infection of the finger.
You couldn't just go someplace warmer
in a helicopter. No wonder Leonardo's
not even sure they are his parents,
he thinks he dropped from a flap
in the cosmos. He thinks if he could
pull a man apart and reassemble him,
the man could fly. Most of what we know
about Leonardo's brain is conjecture
because when the Egyptians pickled him,
all the other organs were carefully
packed in nitron and surrounded by
mummified cats but the brain
was tweezered out and discarded.
In some cultures, eating the brains
of your ancestors is the polite thing to do.
Once in a drive-in, I ate approximately
one ninth of a brain sandwich which
tasted like the meat of sad and horrifying
dreams, the kind you'd have if
you were completely wrapped in bandages
or dropped from a flap in the cosmos.
My girlfriend then could play the piano

without any training at all.
So for awhile the song passing through
our heads seemed passing through
everyone's head then only ours
then only mine then it wasn't a song,
it was a mechanism, part tank, part bellows,
and I got out of there quick.

Mortal Poem

I do not understand why I love you.
The mustard in your hair? Your breasts
like shiny battleships, your thought control?
Reasons seem so insufficient, reason itself
seems insufficient. The sea rushes up
to the beach of no reason, inveigling
chimes for no reason, greenery recumbent
upon the landscape of no reason.

Within the mountain is a valley, within
the blue sky a red one. I don't understand

the weather although I am heavy thralled.
Scraping the windshield made me late, fog
makes me first, cloud shaped like Africa
and I never arrive. Lightning must be
very quick to do its job, otherwise
it'd illumine nothing, pound no chest,
put no lips to unbreathing mouths.

There is an inner weather and an outer weather.
Within the seed is the hundred-year-old tree.
Within the eye an arrow, the heart a storm
while outside it's warm and bony.
It is a mistake to think

everything is inside one's head. Always
darkness somewhere, giraffes with blue
tongues and who could have thought of that?
Opals dissolve in ordinary water, being
part water themselves. When inside the opal,

I often dream I'm swimming, when inside
you, I'm a flood. When inside the jail cell,

I wasn't in full comprehension although
all seemed one clear instance of form
matched to function: lidless toilet
merged with a slab you can sit
or lie upon, floor with a drain somewhere
toward the middle, all one poured

stone unlike the butterfly.

The anvil must be very hard
to do its job but what flies off
isn't sparks, it's pomegranates,
peach blossoms, sharks, it's the beginning

of the world and we are not the hammer swung
but what's under. O my darling, last night
I woke with pain in my chest but
it is gone this morning.

Arts of Camouflage

After years of walking funny,
of sleeping sideways like a shrub,
of trying to transform myself into a panther,
the morning I woke transformed into a panther
wasn't all that different from waking transformed
into a jellyfish, dune grass, into nothing at all.
Same sun in the eyes, same clouds bleeting
like lambs, bleeting like lions eating lambs,
same stupid choice of shirts:
blue or brown,
would I be hiding in sky or ground
which finally didn't matter much
because I tore them all apart. This was in '42.
We felt pretty routy in '42.
There was the war. There was stacking stuff
upon the endless courseways. Nobody was eating
chocolate, then suddenly chocolate was okay.
There was deferment, inkblots, obscure
forestries. The Effort. Kids today,
they look at a rock and think nothing,
think a rock can't just rise up and smote.
There wasn't all this equipment you see advertised
even in commercials about killing ants.
Still we carried plenty.
Detonators. French letters. Atropine.
Philosophy tracts. A thing is never fully itself
but often talks to itself in code.
You'd dream you were surrounded by torn-open bodies
and wake surrounded by torn-open bodies until
the spiritual seemed a preferable dwelling
but purely in a terrifying manner like a leaf

falling from a tree or a stranger
speaking your name.
Sure, I believe in life after death,
it's just that this life after death
is so much like the last one, no one notices
they've already died bunches of times. Same
trenches. Corrosive fogs. Same protective coatings
nearly impossible to get off and when you do,
you've damaged what's inside. Actually I never
changed into a panther. I just said that
to get your attention like someone yelling Fire
when there's really not even a spark,
in fact it's rained solid for weeks.

Lives of the Painters

When I hatched from my black egg,
I ate as many of my brothers and sisters
as I could and got big.
They would have done the same.
But who am I?
Never do I want to see my mother again.
When you want something, that means
you're injured. My father, who I never
want to see again, said he didn't think
I crawled enough so he ripped my gold filter
but then gave me fifteen pairs of suede gloves.
Now I like to fall down hard.
You could be the one for me.
More and more I am saddest in summertime.
Once I planted a peony to surprise someone
I thought cared for me. Now I can't
turn my head suddenly to the left
when pulling erraticly into the passing lanes
because erraticly is how energy behaves
when you put it in too tight a hive.
There's something wrong with my connective tissue.
My T cells are very mad.
But there is no end to treatment
because the body too is a kind of paper
and darling, how good it would be to blot you out
and catch your expression getting all lofty
with a little crayon. Red leaves growing
all around the wound. Then I'd finally
have something on that son of a bitch
Caravaggio who thinks he's the only one
to look into the face of ecstasy and see

a beggar, a thief, a burning church.
Then to crawl down to the concrete hall
and eat mashed potatoes,
mashed potatoes for every meal!
Then to come back and do it all again
until the volumetric depiction of human form
becomes more and more distorted
as it must when the Renaissance
gives way to the Baroque, as evening
gives way to afternoon: impossible ulnas,
swan sperm, beautiful beautiful bicycles.

Don't Wear That Shirt with Those Pants

One need not weep among the leafless trees,
the fraudulent lakescape with kiosks of conflicting
convocations. Sweet is the wind of nonbeing but
sweeter still the exhalations of a thing vibrating.
Even a rodent. One need not crawl the *whole* way
to the temple or look dipped in honey then rolled
in lint or that your dress was dropped upon you
from a Red Cross helicopter or that cataract
surgery is imminent or Marxist rage or mourning
distraction frog pond lichenous yodel although
each is effective in certain situations. Someone,
a stranger, may hand you a golden key. One song
may be only five notes played 804 times. However,
if you're going to wear that last seven meals
shirt, allow me to suggest these weird sleep
pattern pants. The sense of a wall painted
a single yellow is best offset by red ants
attacking black. Oh my darling, I love
harbors in fog. Feel this slub? Do you
want to fight? Carefully introduce accessories
as there is nothing more troubling than
a human head devoured by jewelry. Please
touch this engorged part. Fanny skip lightly
goes awfully well with slide into base blue.
This useless bullshit, I'm surrounded by
useless bullshit jacket may not work with
allee allee in free shoes although it is
preferable always to be a coreoptic head wound
to a clucking turnabout. Savagery is easily
overemphasized when eating lobster. The unknown
always beckons. Your mother told you that,

or tried to before her mind was fashooshed
as birdseed to celestial swans. There, there,
it happens to all of us. There's no sense
in fearing the unknown, even Socrates agrees
although for him it was merely one toga or another.
But for you, resplendent member of a hick university,
this at least I'm a helluva dancer tie is well
worn loose, speech upon the gallows fashion.
For evening escape, try a black body stocking.
For love, always red. Indeed it would be best
if each was judged solely by what is within
but what's a judgment without a powdered wig?

Unthreatening Gestures

Please secure the cap back on the catsup
snugly. First warm day of spring not
screaming. Not screaming mud in the house,
bugs in the house, not screaming for
more, for less, who's going to clean up
this mess. Who would guess in what high
regard the deaf hold Jimi Hendrix. Not
screaming by the casket although slumping
often effective. Anyone who has slain rabbits
knows the racket they can make. The coat
must be held for the woman unless it is red
in a field of bulls. Screaming children
may be locked in closets for muffling.
Napkins should not be refolded after use.
You may want to practice an ironic manner
to put bystanders at ease before attempting
armed robbery. When the man finally gets
his penis inside the woman, it is after
hours of not screaming. Rain rushes
the gutter which rushes the stream which
rushes the sea which screams. The pulmonary
glaze of late evening is best for gentle
sobbing. Many are the shark's teeth.
When I dropped the pot upon my foot,

I did not scream, baby was asleep.

Chapped Lips

The problem with childhood·
is it's wasted on children.
Look at them all strung together
not being run over by the bus.
They're not nearly scared enough.
Just look how they color,
they think they'll be Matisses forever.
They think you can just get up in the morning
and put on velvet shoes. And they're small,
if they were any smaller you could stick them
to the ceiling like flies but no,
they keep lofting back down
like defeated balloons
but what do they know of defeat?
What do they know of the broken bathysphere?
In their little mittens and hats,
truly they look absorbent,
but just try using one to wipe up a spill
and there are so many spills:
spills that make ducks sick,
spills that dissolve railroads,
spills we don't even know what they're doing
but they're sure doing it.
Try explaining that to a child
and all you get is la la la.
Try getting one to sit for an hour
with her face in her hands.
They have almost nothing to remember
so what they forgive could be forgiven
by anyone. They don't pay taxes.
They're completely devoid of pubic hair.

Faculty Summary Report

I'm afraid
they will know how powerless I am
but it is my job to show them

drawings from the asylums, to explain
how a machine gun works, all the functions
of firing and loading done by the gun itself.
And they sit there in waxed hair and crop tops
lip-syncing sitcom jingles in a whirl
of thought oppressed, high on the blithe
ethereal sky wondering if I was ever young.

But then Tania writes her poem rushing to class
and turns it in on a napkin and it's the best
she's ever done and she'll never be able to do it again.
And Mike tells Viola to make her last line
the first and the first the last then
that's her best poem so far.
And in protest of an assignment,
Jennifer just copies stuff about the physiology

of an erection from her nursing text
and that's her best poem ever,
but she feels she didn't even write it
so she turns in a poem about a plane wreck
but no one can tell it's about a plane wreck.

Doug writes only about God and none
of his poems are ever any good which seems
unfair. Two students who live together
say the appearance of Ernesto in their poems

the same week is an accident. Everyone wants
to know who Ernesto is but he isn't anyone
then Tim suddenly gets combative

and misses a class and does nothing
the rest of the semester except dye his hair
and write a poem in the voice of Ernesto
who seems stuck somewhere in a
greenhouse/discotheque/racecar.
Ping ping go the dancers, ding ching the pistons,
kaboom the clouds but what is it the heart goes?
Are we trying to get the tangible to shimmer

or the intangible shimmer to be like wet grass
to push our faces in? Just try being a window
and not taking a hammer to yourself. Even
a harp has obligations. When asked
how long you should practice, Robert Fripp said

eight hours a day and when asked how
people with jobs and lives could do that
said some people can practice eight hours
in fifteen minutes, others it takes years.

Some people think it's important to count
and they're the ones mostly in control.
Some people think it's important to talk

on the radio. To address the situations
of the globe. One poison is so powerful,
a single drop on your finger will kill you
in less than an hour, then kill the people
who come to pick you up. I guess it soaks in

then back out. Last night, I dreamed
I was at a mushy desk surrounded by bales
of student poems. It was my fault
my love had been transformed into a giant

paperclip. My fault Apollinaire, his head
in bandages and dying, trembles in the feverish
victory cries rising from the street. The war
is over but one brain hemisphere thinks
the cries are for him, one thinks it's not

victory at all.
The first thing I always say is
you have to pay attention to your surroundings.
To the car with a canoe strapped to its roof
idling in front of a stone house
with an immense white door.
To the trail in the dew
where something was dragged then taken into the air.

The Oversight Committee

It has always been our intention
that your stay among us be but brief
even though we may have chased you
through the hallways, promised you
our chariot, turned you into echoes
and trees and stars. Oh how you glowed
by the water coolers. As regards
earlier memos re: orgasm cultivation,
that should have read orchid cultivation.
Our apologies particularly to Cheryl
at processing. Still the smear
of your unrunkled sex steams
like monks' illumination upon our thigh.
The mind at such times works wonderfully,
it becomes its own employment which
research on the brains of gazelles
crushed in lions' jaws indicates
is the result of a single neurotransmitter
reserved for just such moments
and finally, isn't it all about moments
jumping other moments, your love for us,
our love for your fur? But later, when someone
calls down the stairs, If you're coming up,
could you bring the tape? none of it
will seem remotely possible: tape,
finding the tape, stairs, climbing the stairs.
The brain has let you down, it thinks,
Why are you still around? Asked for a simple
accounting, many of you submitted poems
about abysses. Only one among you,
asked for a spanner, could actually

produce a spanner. This gives us little choice.
Think of all those flamingos that die each year.
Have courage. Think of all those colored stones
in aquariums. Who knows what happens to them
once the fish are flushed. Holding one's breath
is fine for hurrying through a room
full of poisonous gas but it's not something
we can take to stockholders. Shiny conveyances
have been spotted in the sky, ditto, swans,
all suggesting it is best you move on.
Not every motion falls under our aegis
but for those of you with difficulties
feeding yourselves, a form is being prepared.
Now go, we will always be farther and farther
behind you. Never will we ride an elevator
without thinking of your ass. Finally, don't
forget to turn in your key to Cheryl

and remember, due to the flood,
the tornado drill has been postponed.

Bay Arena

When I worked in the bookstore in Berkeley,
upstairs some woman would sing, alluring
as lava, husky as tar, sometimes it'd be
a whole band driving us a little crazy
downstairs because even good music
heard through a ceiling gets nerve-wracking,
a constant strain to make a whole of it,
catch the lyrics slurred by plumbing prattle
and footfall like you're getting complicated
directions over a bad connection or trying
to figure out just why it is you can't
divide by zero. But I'd say to Michelle
who did the ordering and sometimes would
ask me should she order *The Wasps of*
Puerto Rico, 55 bucks a shot, and I'd say
No way, it'll rot on the shelf like
everything else in Latin America
what with the jungle, poverty, and burn off,
so she'd order three and they'd sell
immediately. More stuff to mess up the store.
I hated customers, how they charged in, tusks
dismantling the alphabet, ranting, raving
in the thick accents of demand, something
about Puerto Rico, something about wasps
as if I was wired individually to each book
and in back, they're stuffing *Treasuries*
of Haiku in their pants, ripping covers off,
who knows, twice I found empty flaps, volumes
by Ricoeur who said I think, Everything is
profoundly cracked, although it might have been
an epigraph he used by someone else because

that's all I ever got to read, an education
of pithy, lost snippets, always trying to do
a million things at once, our filing system
like something out of Kafka, smudgy
index cards organized by press, don't mix up
a slash with a check, so I'd have to explain
and search through *Books in Print* because they'd
forgotten their glasses but really they were
people looking for books who couldn't read!
So I'd say to Michelle in the quiet hour
between 3 and 3:15, Man, that girl can sing,
and she'd just uh-huh because she too lived
upstairs and even Pavarotti would get sickening,
all that passion coming through a wall when
you just want to eat your green beans, watch
a little TV. I mean all music verges on pure
irritation, noise, wearying, weary. Michelle
feeding her turtle ripped up lettuce. Turtle
called Myrtle of course who it was okay
to bring to work, at least she wasn't breast-
feeding at the front desk the way L did who
was finally fired not only for not doing a thing
but fouling up everyone else. I mean there you are,
trying to calm a customer and she opens her blouse,
ladles out this enormous breast, it had a tendency
to knock out everything from anyone's head.
Eternally nonplussed creature, I mean this
turtle who I liked all right but how close
can you get to a turtle? It pulls its
head in, pushes it out, blinks—mostly
I worried about stepping on it then
some guy comes in waving a jar of Prego,
screaming about the New Deal and, This is it,
I think, I will die in Berkeley in a splatter

of extra thick sauce, a corona of glass
spread out like my incomplete poems,
my brains spilled out like sensibility
as outside the street starts percolating
in the gelling light. Soon the protesters
will be throwing rocks at the gym because
a volleyball court's finally gone into
People's Park like the university's been
threatening to do through the ages of Aquarius
and later cops shooting wooden pegs but
that afternoon I'm getting my falafel
lunch at the caboose on Bancroft from
the guy who always asks me how I'm managing
and tells me how he's sleeping, not too
good, who could these days, and I say Amen,
handing over my 2.25, giving this Arab
a more mixed message than I intend and
the guy in the tutu and evening gloves,
the Love-Hate man with rouge in his beard
is matching the blustering fundamentalist
syllable by syllable: for every hell a bell,
every damnation a dalmatian, shadow for
shadow, wagging Bible against wagging
New Age Singles, satori, samsara, and then
I hear her like smoke my mother blew in
my ear when I had an earache and I strain
against what lashes me to the mast. *We are*
stardust, we are golden, and there she is.
She must weigh 300 pounds, head like a glop
of Playdoh dropped on a mountain of smoldering
hams, feet immense puddles in those specially
designed fat shoes that lace on both sides
and that voice like a swan hatching from
a putrid egg and people tossing change

into a tambourine, arrhythmic accompaniment
to the drummer who closes his eyes,
the guitarist who closes his eyes,
the music passing through us all like
some frail filament driven through a pole
during a hurricane, through all our barriers
of tissue toward outer space, the rapacious
gardens of stars from which we've fallen,
shuddering cores of cinder, whirlwinds of ash.

Myth Mix

In the beginning, everything is mingled
and joined, all the halves hooked up,
nothing reft or twain, no missing buttons,
no single baby shoes lying by the off-ramps.
In the beginning everything's combined
smaller than a grapefruit and that's the first
happiness which makes all the later happinesses
like threads snagged from a tapestry.
So fine: everything's all smashed together
but then along comes coyote and pisses on it
then the ticking starts and the dark arabesques,
the scarlet wheels and none of us can get
far enough away from each other
and none of us can get close enough
so these two desires lie on top of each other
and make more desires but some come out
mangled, missing wings, with angry mouths.
They're the despairs. So all these desires
and despairs are zipping around looking for
parking spaces, crashing into each other
so it's like a big party with ambulances
where some signifiers are weeping in the bushes,
some are eating the cake's giant sugar rose,
and one drinks too much ambrosia and vomits
Jimi Hendrix so the violinists drop their bows
and pick up bolt cutters which helps make pain
beautiful and later more and more gold hammers
are called in to make pain really beautiful.
Which gets Zeus's attention so he throws down
some lightning bolts which is pretty much
his response to everything, vaporizing some

cheerleaders but mostly just blasting holes
in the ground which people use as basements
for buildings where they go and invent ways
to kill dandelions that also kill ants and
the warblers who eat the ants then the warblers
fall into the river and the river loses consciousness
and has to be put on life support. Then the nurse,
who is trying to raise two boys and actualize
herself, one night opens a window in the river's
semiprivate room and there's the Void.
Uh-oh. She feels pretty dumb opening
a window on the Void but now she can't
get it closed and it's making a high
lisping she can't get out of her head so
she tells her group and they try to sympathize
but each is obviously relieved not to be
that fucked up. So she gets used to it,
starts to hum along a little and the place
is looking tidier and she feels almost relaxed.
Those appointments—what were they?
But all this time the universe is flitting
away, cotton swab by cotton swab,
salamander by salamander, Woolworth's,
old movie stars, whole blocks of the town
she was born in and the window keeps
getting wider until it's a whole wall,
the ward, East and by then everyone
who's left can feel things missing
but not what, just a sense of empty
velvet-lined indentations, sighs in halls,
tissue paper, loose chains clanking in streets
that lunge into the fog and then there's a lurch
and the word *lurch* floats off the last page
leaving behind a single blue line then

the line becomes a dot and the dot becomes
a hole and no one knows if that's the first
happiness come back or not but you won't have to
lie, your hands won't swell up, you won't
have to pee into a plastic cup, blood
won't fill your mouth as strangers
ask you your name. You won't have to carry
anything. It will be like sleeping and
you won't have to worry if you are really loved.

three

Guidance Counseling

(AFTER BRETON AND ELUARD)

When the woman, her shoulders on the bed,
lifts her pelvis into the standing man,
it is called Dentist Office. When the man,
after an hour hiding in a closet, couples
with she of the silk flowered dress, snug
in the bodice, it is called Representational
Democracy. When the woman licks her burnt
finger, Tiny Garden Hose. Often, as we grow
old, life becomes a page obscured with
too many words like the sea with too many
flashes. Like my screaming may obscure
my love for you. How will we ever understand
each other? When the woman sits on the ladder
and the man churns like a lizard, stiff
in melting ice cream, it is called Many Dews.
If the man is able to lie on his stomach
and somehow penetrate the woman who lies
on top of him while she devours his head,
it is called Preying Mantis. In the event
of a water landing, your seat becomes
a flotation device. What happens continues
to happen more or less until we die
in some sudden or slow way. It may be
Bull Fight, it may be Wind in the Trees.
You will need at least two dressy outfits,
one for rehearsal, the other for actual.
When the woman pushes the man down in a chair,
rubs her breasts in his face and all
is rich and fleeing, risen and slain,
enmeshed in the hour's russet locks, surged,

wet with, it is called Laughing Inside the Go,
called Cathedral Hidden or Cloud Done, Long
or Sudden Done, Last Exhausts Blown to Sea,
Tolling of Everything Empty, Diamond Empty,
Chest After Sobbing and when the woman
is combing and the man is asleep, when
the woman enters an elevator, a gentleman
removes his hat.

Safe Sex

Often you'll feel two things at once
powerfully at odds as when in love
one wants to spend all day in bed
yet also jump up and buy a mop!
How good it feels to make toast!
and to think about death, how

in the ground, the newly buried
take on such riotous expressions.
Even the living you shop among
seem decomposing like old lemons.
Oh, you're young again, the film
is running backwards. Look, water

leaps out of the tub, blood crawls
back into the cut, the secret's licked
out of the ear which accounts, in part,
for the struggle as the woman tries
to pat and calm her dog while the man
ransacks her body. Often in your search

you'll find you're hiding something.
A warning hangs over the glistening
compartments and the woman cries out
like a harp because either the harp
that's inside her is being plucked
or the harp that's outside her

is dropped. Please try to be careful.
In these moments, scissors are particularly
poignant, so too the reflectors of trucks

passing in the rain. There is a nervousness,
an ache. Slowly and suddenly, it's
the end of the parade, the part anyone

can join if he or she has a wagon, lavish
boots, some wound or any manner of need
for public display and those trucks —
surely half are empty. So one kisses
the legs not for the first time, ejaculates
among the cabbage palm fronds way back

already in an aboriginal song, everything
already done and gone and yet each afternoon
one wakes always for the first time,
throws back the curtains on always new
mountains, never the same radio tower,
never the same darling percolated in dream.

One day every day all that will be left
is ash and ash completely a-throb, flushed
and without relief because the body hungers
to be ash, to eat ash the way clouds hunger
for mountains to smash against so they
no longer have to be clouds, a sort

of suicide the way the rain throws itself
into the river, the river throws itself
into you because sometimes the loneliness —
or is it joy — is unbearable.

A Student in a Distant Land

We could see some mountains I didn't
know the name of where some adventurers
had recently gone to freeze to death.
She said, Our lives are but torn bits
of party hats blown by breezes of the sea.
I said, When with I lousy swordfish.
My boat would be arriving soon, blasting
gas from itself. In the charming way
of this place, small children dressed
as trees kept running up to sell us
hunks of coal decorated with teeth.
Wool, she said, is an excellent source
of income for these islanders. I said,
Thrumming skylight, bridge of will-you.
We had known each other but a short time
yet my love for her, like a coat hung
from a nail, resembled me in ways I
did not resemble myself as if something
dear had been reft from me only to be
restored with the matchbooks of hotels
I'd never been to in its pockets. Your pain,
she murmured, your future, your rope burns.
Her body, under the massive yak hide, glistened
like a wet yo-yo. Agg tag glatmoogen,
I approximated in her native tongue but
it could not staunch the tears. The clouds
were bells. I wilth always lube you,
she sobbed, but I mush return hushbang
of factory. Vulcanization is the process
by which rubber fibers are brought into

alignment conferring elasticity but how,
how? With sulphur. I know that now.
And sometimes hydrogen peroxide.

Another Hive

for Barry Hannah

What was I doing last night talking about Flaubert
in the French restaurant when I don't understand
a thing about Flaubert, not the long description
of the knot of hair, not how many drafts
the broken fingernail scene went through.
I had never been to Paris many times
but none impressed me as much as this.
My food seemed to have died from abstract speculation.
You had to speak as if your lips would do anything
to leave your face. How can you trust a culture
that never passed through a gladiatorial age?
Barry kept saying, No one who wasn't a pilot
would ever understand. Even the word *potato*
sounded ethereal but from what I know of the ethereal,
it's not any place to get a sensible meal.
It is spring. A rock falls upon us,
we cry out but sometimes it's not
even a corporeal rock, it's a spirit rock,
a rock made of ourselves. Hey Barry,
how's your lamb? No one who wasn't a pilot
would understand. The heart lifts and rolls.
The names of perfumes are all puns conflating
coitus with space travel. Some nights,
I'd just lie in bed wondering what a boy
from Jersey whose father inspected picture tubes
wasn't doing in Paris ejaculating grasshoppers
into the gutter of some book I couldn't stop
writing. Sometimes I'd just bite my hand
to make sure I wasn't made of balsa wood.
But, over the semester, as I didn't go

to Paris more and more, the feeling faded
like the drawing of a bunny in soft lead
I keep taking out of my wallet to remind myself
of the talent God gave me. Now, I'm just one
of a dozen penitents at museum receiving
unloading the fucking heavy art. Later,
the whole idea will be to get you
to forget the thing weighs tons
which was one of the church's ideas
and the other was to kill you.

Robert Desnos (1900–1945)

A surrealist in the twenties, praised
by Breton for dictating epigrams while
asleep. Others were met by servants
with torches and informed they too
were servants. Broke with Breton in 1930
over a description of the sex organs
of a starfish. It rained. The plain
and lower hill were covered with hoplites
only pretending to be wounded. Gears
made bouquets in the air until the clouds
became grease. Meanwhile, Desnos wrote
radio plays for children and made himself
a vest of ice. He'd forgotten he should
have been screaming. The chains and nets
around him formed layer upon interlocking
layer until the entire work force became
a cylindrical mass. *I have dreamed of you
so often, you are no longer real,* he
dictated but then what was always real
became realer, the stitch made longer
or shorter by a varying eccentric stroke.
He held up a broken doll in the street,
trying to make it sing. During the war,
Desnos stole small silver bells for
the Resistance. In the gyroscope,
momentum and the rotational axis
preserve their direction as long as
no external force acts upon it but
how long do you think that could last?
Arrested by the Gestapo and sent to
Buchenwald in April, blood filled

his lungs shortly after liberation.
He drowned in the middle of a dirt road,
his remains identified only by the words
shining on his forehead: *shadow*
moves on and goes on moving, brightly
over the sundial of our lives.

Archeology

The wren says, Let's fly really fast
then veer sharply but the man just sits.
The kettle says, Let's just sit here and
get really really mad but the man's
been reading about ruins again and

he wants one of his own. Maybe just
a jaw to put on his desk to fondle
and think, Miraculous and what's the point.
Also it's May so the man goes outside
and starts digging and soon he's uncovered

what looks like the top of a stone head.
Let's rest a while, says the music
coming from the radio then, Let's
crash an airplane into the Everglades
but by now the man's realizing he's

started another thing he doesn't want
to finish and the hole is shouting,
Something's in me, get it out! So
after a couple root-popping, clay-
prying hours, he's exposed a whole face,

pupils plugged with mud, lips straight
as if the teeth are meeting beneath.
The neck, he has to use his hands
to get to the neck, it's two strong
tendons and then what he hopes aren't,

but are, shoulders. Let's forget all
about this and explode our brains, propose
the daffodils. Watch what I can do
with my shadow, says a tree, spooky huh?
But the man's wondering about this thing's

expression, is it about to laugh or
pass some terrible judgment? And what
about the arms? Holding a spear, scroll,
lyre, some farm implement? Already
he's bleeding when all he wanted

was some fragment as a sort of proof
like the moth wings a woman sent him proved
she never wanted to see him again. What
kind of reasoning is that, asks the garbage
truck, gnawing. What do you know about

perishing? There's always this point when
he becomes engulfed in extravagances and
nearly too dirty to walk into his own house.
Let's eat mud and make mud, suggest the worms.
Let's be nothing but big bellies above

the planet, advise the clouds but the man
knows he's got weeks of work ahead, he needs
to find out if he's got some god here
or just another swindling dignitary,
he needs to know if this is the king

everyone's supposed to worship, the one
the taxes flow to from this weedy
province where we've nearly given up

all our appropriate dread. Horses
in the night, glittering breastplates

of thunder, red eyes blinking
on the radar weather maps, tell me
who I am, tell me what I've become.

Drinking from a Puddle

Denise says she can't recall one decent fuck
from the five years of her first marriage
and this wine isn't dry enough either.
When she finally goes to the bathroom,
the second husband whispers it's Laura's
birthday and she's probably in India now.
This morning I woke thinking about purity
again. If I could get the loan and that place
on the hill in Berkeley, each morning I'd
go out on the deck in muddy sandals left
by the door and look for rattlesnakes
slow in the fog. Maybe pick one up.
My pure life. Always about to begin.
Then I remembered Duke Sapp moving
everything I owned in his pickup
when we were students, one load,
three trips up two flights to the room
by the carillon, how I'd never lock it
because I kept losing the key and one night
his girlfriend, drunk, waiting for me
in nothing but my only good white shirt.

Dog Toy

Master, how can I make a million dollars?
Cherry blossoms shake in the rain.
Have you tried decorative switch covers?
Yes, but the process was too expensive
with much breakage. Moon-dabbed
bush clover. Have you tried a dog toy
made from two tennis balls united
by a short length of rappeling rope?
So the novice goes off and does this
very cheaply and sells 35,000 in a week
at 200% above cost then Purina Dog Chow
offers to buy him out for a mill.
But still, as evening collapses
upon the orangeade drinkers carousing
the boutiques, he puts his hand down
his throat to touch his own heart
and it stings. A million isn't
all that much. So he goes back up
to the hut on the mountain and asks,
Is it the lion in the cave or
the lion coming out, roaring?
Neither in nor out, what is that?
suggests the Master. But isn't there
something more, pleads the novice.
Have you tried love? taunts the Master.
So the novice goes back to Berkeley
and eats crab with an undergraduate
who makes him feel in danger but
also volcanic, the crab cracks like fire,
her breasts shine like the sea glimpsed
through a broken wall but he's afraid

she won't leave and at the same time
afraid she won't stay and she keeps saying
she wants to be an aromatherapist so
the novice decides he must quit this world
and give everything he owns to a group
protecting the coyote. There are two kinds
of people and the right ones think it's okay
if a coyote eats the occasional chihuahua.
So the novice returns and says I have done
everything you said. What things? explains
the Master. There is no doing, no not doing.
No two kind of people. There is only the fluid
that drips from the dragon's mouth.
But what about the effect of glucosamine
on synovial joints? People actually say
they feel better. What about Beethoven's
deafness, cunnilingus, what is the best way
to cook fish? Cover with wax paper and marinate
for two hours then saute rapidly in hot
olive oil. Do you have any spare change?
proposes the Master. But what about
walking in the rain and being miserable,
what about being happy with nothing,
how the clouds that are nothing completely
consume the mountain? And they go on like this
for years, learning nothing, sleeping late,
getting drunk until the Master dies
like snow melting from a fence. So
the novice writes a book called *Dog Toy*
that becomes a bestseller then he goes
on a talk show with someone who fell
from an airplane and survived and
someone else who had been struck
by lightning many times and survived

and a woman who had exhausted all
conventional treatment but when
all hope seemed gone,
she just started concentrating
and drinking a lot of water
until she was completely healed
and able to move paperclips without
even touching them. What are you
waiting for? You've already
been given your free gift.

Agony in the Garden

Today my friend asks me if I want
to pull weeds all afternoon but I can't
because the Lineaments of this World
Feather Out into the Cosmos as Blake

keeps burning into his plate which
makes of any weed-pull a struggle
with the infinite and I'm struggling
with the next couple hours as it is.

Something ciliated keeps rushing toward me
but not getting any closer and I
don't think I want it any closer.
My friend says everything ends up

a congress of wasps anyway. His yard,
his job, his marriage. He and his wife
still sleep together but each time
it's devastation and as soon as the kid's

off to school, he'll move out. And to think
he used to do her laundry in his aorta.
Sometimes, though, the organism may look
dead when really it's only stunned.

You can watch it blaze right out of itself
with a little acid prodding. Sun
upon coiled rope, goofy cadmium corpi
proclaiming their existence like the wackos

on the boulevards with their tragic cardboard.
The Matter of this World is Fiercely Bound
with Energy and is Eternal. Sure it is.
Imagine being locked inside a lightbulb.

Just think of how much you'd like it in there!
Never having to watch your mouth!
The lousy table service! A rosebush
instead of sexual organs! But my friend

says everything burns out and no one
can be protected. Finally the buzzing
stops and someone comes in with a mop.
How understandable it all is, how dependent

upon radius of raindrop, hue, swirls
of protoplasm, and a spark then the creature
rights itself and starts singing country western.

The Velvet Underground

Everyone's sitting around Nick's and Kenny says,
The Velvet Underground was the first,
and then everyone realizes Dan's not there
because he would say, No, so and so was the first,
someone no one's heard of. Expect periods
of rain and becoming breezy. Maybe he's found
a girl. She backed her tornado into his wind chime.
Raspberry sherbet. How long's it been since
anyone's seen him? No one can precisely recall
yet Dan is still quite exact like the first time
a shrimp is brought to you on a plate with
its head still attached. His equipage unslurred
in the holy mud. Of all the speakers of French
among us, Dan sounds the most alert whatever he's saying:
The young lady's undergarments rued with tragic
surmise, or Please, porter, *avaunt*. It always sounds
convincing. A recipe for croutons. Still,
there is also a sense of openness, uncertainty
as when one carries a cup too full of something
hot, or makes eye contact with the zooed
lioness, or finds a twenty in an old pocket.
That sound during one song turns out to be
the guy playing viola scraping a metal chair.
Gee, I hope he doesn't have his head in an oven,
says Erin. On a timeline in which a year is
a foot, Dan and Erin's coupledom would be
a quarter inch long but ten thousand miles high.
She doesn't know ten years ago Dan was so wrecked
over a librarian, his head in fact was put
in an oven only to realize it was an electric oven
thereby beginning the life of the next Dan,

the one everyone knows for his argumentative
sense of the absurd, who no one can imagine
with his head in the oven except Kenny who can
imagine anyone thus. Job liability. And jumping off
a bridge and opening a wrist in a warm tub
listening to chamber music. Are his parents
still alive? Doesn't he know someone who owns
property in the mountains? Maybe I should call,
says Kenny, unmoving. The theory of cloud
formation, theory of mimetic desire, market
transfer. Is he writing a book? Everyone's
writing a book. Barometric pressure, prewar
shortages, bloused breezes of whiskeyed spring—
nothing holds us for long. So many friends
yet one remains unknown.

The Woman Who Parks in Front of My House

hair the color of red vinyl talking
to a guy who's walked his 10-speed
to be with her the six blocks from campus.
On the outside their mouths discussing
maybe Brad failing or the condition of
those manuscripts the weird weather
glucagon the king who liked locks.
Many many forces. Some say never wear
this shirt with these pants again.
It is very likely the foot-dragging
bishop Tallyrand was the illegitimate
father of Eugene Delacroix, painter of
Napoleon and Napoleon's horse. What
was the name of Napoleon's horse?
That's what the mouths on the outside
are doing but when she finally gets in
her ulcerated Jetta, Gimme gimme gimme,
orates the radio for a second. Achilles
and Agamemnon glare at each other and
all the other generals think, We really
are going to be here forever. All those
little bones of the wrist. Gotta gotta
gotta. Then she drives off and you can
see by the way he leans against the deranged
stratosphere that there was some other
conversation that hadn't gotten out,
an inner question and now, while he
looks at the cracks above as if the sky
was a poorly preserved painting of the sky
with an entirely different sky beneath,
the answer seems to be No. All that's left

of one spell on papyrus DB-76 is "soak
the donkey head in milk." Do not order
eggplant in the steakhouse, he could be
repeating to himself, do not expect
the titration to take care of itself,
knowing full well that again and again
at the end of the day he will follow her
through the big doors and maybe once
his shirt will be right, maybe eggplant
will be exactly the thing that most
baby baby baby beautifully arrives.

God Son

What could the baby know the couple
laterals back and forth, it's a thing
with a hundred wings, half snake, half
bag of smoke, clutching, kicking off,
swallowing the universe and about to

spit it up. They're sitting in chairs
chained together so no one can steal
one at a time. The baby's only about
22 by 10 by 9 inches thick but already
their present house isn't enough,

the bending porch, back room full
of torn cocoons. Head barely attached,
he's yet to crash even a kite, Fortinbras's
yet to mince through the corpses stacked
like blank verse on the stage but already

in his brow one detects a refined sense
of the tragic. Tragedy—tramp of the goat's
hoof. Maybe one day he'll brew a new serum
to help the sick hop out of bed, maybe compose
an opera that lets the jaded forget

their mortgage payments, their parents'
protracted and expensive deaths. Still,
he'll always have this other gift,
he'll look at the waves and know which
is most tragic, the one throwing itself

too soon upon the sand I can't go on,
one rushing up with the remnants of
butchered dolphins stuck to its tress.
A hundred planets, a thousand eyes,
fear and hope, fear and hope

spinning above the bassinet.

Three Weeks Late

Because they've forgotten they're slaves,
the man and woman are lying in bed,
windows open, curtains closed. Outside,
an enormous variety of birds, none
saying remotely tweet. Hacksaw underwater,
little helpless-without-you.
On one hand they're two gods agreeing
to appear entirely human, on the other
there's no agreement at all.
Under all these bandages, where're
the pharaohs? Alternately, they sit,
arch, phosphoresce, satellite upon each other,
their masks so slippery with goo they smack
back onto the face, stinging it, bringing
tears to the eyes. Tears to the eyes
in the realm of the irreversible which means
here come the spurned others,
one he left crying, one she told the truth
and left shouting. They stick for a moment
to the walls like wet crepe paper
but then the sun scours them away.
In DeKooning's big red picture,
there's a slaughter of the visible
but the visible fights back and wins.
Because it wants to go on forever?
Silly thing that wants to go on forever.
And because they're not sure if they'll ever
wake, the man and woman are still lying in bed.
Black lacquer box full of jewels. A novel
with a forest fire at its core. Let's

paint your kitchen tomorrow, says the man.
I'm already asleep, answers the woman
but then the phone rings and when they get up
to not answer it, there's all this blood on the sheet.

Easily Bruised

Sometimes the foramen ovale doesn't
close and because this baby only lived
an hour on a hose, we are in this airy
church. Sometimes it's hard to think
we die just once. Maybe the world
floats through the cosmos on
a turtle's back. Maybe it's held
in an eagle's beak. But it's certain
a million things can go wrong.
For the ancient Greek girl,
a shower of gold might impregnate her
or she might become a tree instead,
trying to avoid the whole mess.
It is bad enough if a god ignores you,
far worse to call down one's love
so why aren't we more careful
being beautiful? Some of the women
in silk dresses sob. The men position
umbrellas downward, collapsed and dripping.
Sometimes for the ancient Greek,
the baby emerged with characteristics
not entirely human. A gift or curse?
Happy birthday. The good news is
you'll be able to foretell the future,
the bad that you'll never be believed.
It makes of everything a warning.
Why one cell decides to make an eye
and not a horn is one of embryology's
biggest riddles. More than a million
things can go wrong and because
this baby only lived an hour,

we are in this airy church. Hear
our prayer, oh Lord? Outside
there are flowering plum trees
beside the gashed earth.
There is the fact of any god's savagery.
In a couple hours, the organist
will play a wedding march.
In 90 years another baby born this day
will be like a baby again, curled up in bed,
easily bruised while all around
dart milky parallelograms,
the fiery triangles
charged with her protection.

Lives of the Poets

To you, Walt Whitman has probably
always been dead but to me he died
just yesterday after many pages,
his body a mess, large portions
nearly empty although it was the other parts
filled with masses beyond the understanding
of the 19th century that prevented him
from becoming a wind instrument or a kite
but sometimes he's still a whole orchestra
unto himself as if every word he ever wrote
was being said simultaneously although
a little muffled, maybe just a squirrel
landing on the roof of another world
or a vacuum cleaner hose shifting
among the overcoats of another world
because the life of a poet is always
passing from one world to another, dream
to dream, tissue through tissue, red
stain upon the beach. My friend's solution
is to read me another version of paradise
over the phone. At first the gods lie around
slurping the fruits of the Tree of Knowledge
until they're full but because this is paradise,
they're never full but what they get is
stupefied with the silk and slither of it,
the wet-going-down, oh how they long to
click some ammo in, wreck a bicycle,
anything but every greasy secret unhinged,
every outburst musical as if all singing
didn't come from singeing so finally
they grow intolerable to themselves,

they start to stink and shun each other
until finally (because this is paradise,
it's finally all the time) finally
they fall like frost-bit peaches
back into the mud, the furnace, into—
the lucky ones—the bodies of caterpillars
who spin from themselves the finest filaments.
It's hard to believe how strong silk is
considering it comes from a bug's butt
and often it's quite instructive to try
ripping some parachute, some net, some flouncy
party dress, to try and break these ties
that bind us oh my lord. Imfuckingpossible.
My friend has almost nothing to say
about the woman he loves who stole his furniture,
nothing about the singing children you can't
avoid this time of year. I hate singing
children, as if anything deserves to be so un-
ugly, as if we all aren't on one end or another
of the spear. Ants climbing over ants.
Geese waddling through frozen fields. My friend
has even less to say about Walt Whitman.
Odic force or cosmic wanker? Almost everything
he revised, he made worse. Certainly
his family was a handful. Mom suffered
from rheumatism of the leg variously
diagnosed as Vaporous Ejectum, Crunching
Womb, Salt in the Clusters then she died,
still unable to punctuate sensibly. And Eddy,
retarded, mostly confined younger brother,
came to resemble the flyleaf portraits
of the bard more than he did himself
those waning years. Eddy, however,
responded only to sweets. Led into his rooms

those waning years, you'd be greeted
by the Kosmos enveloped in white sheets
unable to get up from the piles of papers
he forbade his housekeeper (who
would have to sue for back wages)
to touch. Little wound, little wound,
what is it you wish to say? You think
you'll recover but you'll never recover.
I was drunk when I got here, I plan
on being drunk when I leave.

Acknowledgments

Thanks to the editors of these magazines in which some of these poems were first published: *Agni Review* ("Colophon"); *American Poetry Review* ("Myth Mix"); *Burning Car* ("Unthreatening Gestures"); *Colorado Review* ("Three Weeks Late"); *Crazyhorse* ("God Son," "The Unattainable"); *Gettysburg Review* ("Dog Toy," "Easily Bruised," "The Woman Who Parks in Front of My House"); *Harvard Review* ("Archeology" and "Chapped Lips"); *Iowa Review* ("Bird Sanctuary" and "If Thou Dislik'st What Thou First Light'st On"); *New American Writing* ("The Infirmament" and "Warbler"); *Ohio Review* ("Because Her Face" and "Tiger"); *Sycamore Review* ("Bay Arena" under the title "First Course in Turbulence"); *Third Coast* ("Mortal Poem" and "The Velvet Underground"); *Three Penny Review* ("Acceptance Speech," "Lives of the Inventors," "Lives of the Poets"); and *TriQuarterly* ("The Oversight Committee").

Thanks to the National Endowment for the Arts for a fellowship during the writing of this book.

Thanks to these friends who helped: Roger Mitchell, David Rivard, David Wojahn, Keith Ratzlaff. Brenda Hillman and Robert Hass. Wendy Lesser. Joe DiPrisco. Bob King. Dobby Gibson, Karen Carcia, and James D'Agostino.

And my brother Tony Hoagland.